Disclaimer:

Every effort has been made to check the contents of this book for accuracy. However, the authors recommend that the student always consult their supervisor before making any changes. The information used and decisions taken are entirely at your own risk. Project thesis structures and content maybe required differently at some institutions or courses. The contents of this book are based on the authors' research. The authors cannot be held responsible for the results of action, inaction, or otherwise taken as a consequence of the information in this book. All the Internet addresses (URLs) contained within this book are valid at the time of going to press. However, due to the dynamic nature of the Internet, some addresses may change and some sites may alter or cease to exist, post publication. Whilst the authors and publishers regret any inconvenience this may cause readers, either the authors or publishers can accept no responsibility for any such changes.

Final Year Project Thesis

Foreword

"After over sixty years in Higher Education it is a pleasure to welcome another book about Final Year Projects.

There is indeed a plethora of literature on this topic, much of it specific to particular courses or institutions. Usually it is useful, often worthy, frequently good, but eye-opener examples are rare.

Here I believe we may have one such. Not because of any flashy heterodoxy, but by its comprehensive clarity, logical sequencing, confident handling of statistical materials and accessibility, mirroring the professional expertise, wide experience and student empathy of the author. It provides an ideal template for successful submission.

A boon to any graduate researcher and equally valuable to their supervisors."

Professor Bartley Culverwell, BSc (Econ) MSc MBA PhD ACP FRAI

Director of Education London Graduate School of Management
Reporting Inspector for the British Accreditation Council for Further and Higher Education in the Private Sector.
Intermittently Head of the Business School University of Greenwich and of Community Education at Dartford College of Education.

Table of Contents

List of Figure:

Section 1. Project structure.

1.1: What is a Final Year Project?

A final year project represents a demonstration of a student's ability to **integrate** the knowledge they acquired from more than one course and subject, to produce a final work that shows their readiness to graduate. In many cases, students are also required to demonstrate the ability to **learn new skills** on their own.

However, the write up of the final year project has to follow clear academic guidelines that also show: **integrity, creativity, organization,** and **research skills.**

Before we start explaining the different sections of a project thesis, a student should confirm with their project supervisor that they are happy with the general structure suggested below. The structure here is a popular academic structure for writing up a final year project used by degree, master's, and even PhD students. This academic structure is not difficult to understand or implement. We recommend students to make a quick review of it before they start and come back to read each section as they write it.

1.2: General Thesis structure:

1. Project Front Page.

2. Abstract.

3. List of Contents.

4. List of Figures.

5. List of Tables.

6. Acknowledgement.

7. Definition of terms.

8. Chapter One: Introduction.

9. Chapter Two: Literature review.

10. Chapter Three: Case Study.

11. Chapter Four: Methodology.

12. Chapter Five: Implementation.

13. Chapter Six: Evaluation.

14. Chapter Seven: Conclusion

15. Bibliography.

16. Appendices.

Please note that the naming of these sections is not

fixed and it is very common that the institution, supervisor, or course may require students to rename or order these titles in different ways.

Once the student decides on their topic, then they should consider looking at similar projects to see how they are sectioned. Even though some projects will have slightly different titles, the content will be the same. For instance for Chapter Two: Literature review, students may find some projects call this chapter: Research, Academic Review, Current literature, Research background, or Review of Research. In essence, these are still called "Literature review". Similarly Chapter Four: Methodology, students may find some project call it: Implementation Plan, Method, or Research Approach. Again in essence, all these names for Chapter Four means the same thing: "How will the student implement the project?"

1.3: Different levels and expectations

Final year projects thesis on the degree, masters, MBA, and PhD has a lot in common. In many cases the structure is almost identical and the difference is almost exclusively in the content level and expected academic outcome.

The expectations from degree students when writing their final year thesis is mostly on their <u>ability to integrate the knowledge</u> they have acquired and applying academic skills in the context of a project thesis. While students may demonstrate some creativity, for the majority of qualifications, this is not essential. The knowledge contribution would be mostly at <u>demonstrating new skills the students acquired</u>. Students are expected to show good academic integrity and research skills.

For example, software engineering students would be expected to create an application for a real company or case study that would not only challenge their skills in writing programming codes but demonstrate their abilities in researching about the topic, designing the systems, network, security, and well as their project management skill.

The expectations from the master degree students when writing their final year masters thesis is to demonstrate their ability to integrate the knowledge they have acquired but to include research skills that shows <u>students have advanced beyond the knowledge acquired</u> in the class to include the latest research in this area. The students are able to integrate knowledge collected from research or from the literature review into their project thesis. <u>Some level of creativity expected in the area of study</u>. The knowledge contribution maybe drawn from the latest literature or research that provides new insights into the student's subject area. Finally, the student is to demonstrate excellent academic integrity and a sound methodology in their thesis.

For example, software engineering students would be expected to identify latest developments in a specific software engineering field, involving a challenging case study, and by doing so create a solution that maybe in part based on the recent research application in improving the system efficiency, design, and/or security.

Finally, the expectations from the PhD students when writing their PhD thesis is to demonstrate all of the skills mentioned before to the highest standards while demonstrating three key criteria: Firstly, they have to prove that there is academic interest in this subject; secondly, the work is original and contributes to knowledge something not done before; thirdly, it is based on sound academic and scientific research methods.

It is, therefore, not totally unheard of that sometimes degree students produce a final year thesis that is considered of such high quality that it would qualify as Masters degree level. There are cases where final year masters and MBA thesis have been deemed as of high quality to qualify as entry level into a PhD thesis. In fact, this is one of the many opportunities that have come about where a student may have done an outstanding work in their Masters degree that they were invited to continue that same research into their PhD. Some universities instruct their supervisors to look out for these bright students for potential PhD scholarships.

1.4: Planning the write up of the project

Another issue to consider here is the sequence of writing these chapters. Students would be mistaken to think that the sequence, while seems logical to read, is the same sequence in which to write the project. For example, the abstract cannot possibly be written or finalize the introduction until the project is completed. Yet those two sections are appear that start of the project. Below is a suggestion on how to plan the sequence of writing the project.

Phase 1: Agreeing the title, aims and objectives, and general structure of the project. Having a general idea on how the project will be conducted and that the expected outcome will be.
    Outcome: Create outline of Chapter One: Introduction.

Phase 2: Conducting extensive literature review on the topics related to the project. Create first draft of the bibliography (references).
    Outcome: Create most of Chapter Two: Literature review and Bibliography.

Phase 3: Where a project has case study, especially business and IT projects, students need to create a detailed case study that demonstrate very good understanding of that case in relation to their project.
    Outcome: Completing Chapter Three: Case study

Phase 4: Deciding how the project will be conducted in relation to the case study or the topic of the research. Appending any literature found on how a project is conducted to Chapter two: Literature review.

> Outcome: Completing the literature review and most of Chapter four: Methodology.

Phase 5: Implementation of the work. Students to implement the research or work they need to do for the project. It is common that new areas are discovered that may influence how the project progresses; including new challenges and new ways to do things. This may require students to go back and add or edit Chapter two: Literature review, Chapter three: Case study, and Chapter Four: Methodology.

> Outcome: Completing Chapter Five: Implementation and updating Chapters two, three and four.

Phase 6: Analysis of the implementation and results, this is particularly important to explain the outcome and if the outcome is incorrect, this may prompt changes in all the previous chapters.

> Outcome: Completing Chapter six: Evaluation and Chapter seven: Conclusion.

Phase 7: Going back to Chapter one: Introduction to reflect changes that have taken place in the original plan, aims, objectives, and project structure.

> Outcome: Completing Chapter one.

Phase 8: Creating the Abstract and Acknowledgment.
   Outcome: Abstract and Acknowledgment.

Phase 9: Reading the project as a whole, ensuring consistency in headings, style, content, message, references, and outcome. Looking for difficult terms and their explanations.
   Outcome: All sections and chapters reviewed. Creating the table of content and definition of terms (optional).

Phase 10: Project Front page and appendix content included.

1.5 Project Meetings

Students should treat meetings with their supervisors as serious as any exam. While supervisors do not necessary grade the student at every meeting, the impression they get from the student and how well they are prepared for each meeting can have profound effect on the way their final project is approached and graded. Two scenarios come to mind from previous experiences.

Scenario 1: A student rarely or never shows up to their scheduled meetings with a supervisor. Two consequences could come up when the supervisor is marking the student's project. Firstly there is the fact that the supervisor will not know or be sure what the project is about and will have to rely on how well the student wrote their project. This is not always easy. Thus the grade will suffer. Secondly where the project is written in an excellent way, with little or no support from the supervisor, then the supervisor will rightly view the work with suspicion of cheating. In fact, this has proved many times to be the case especially when the work is written in style or standards that exceeds the expectations of that level.

Scenario 2: A student regularly attends their scheduled meetings, regularly stays in touch with their supervisor either face-to-face or by email including responding always to the feedback and requests of the supervisor, then the supervisor would approach their final project knowing exactly what the work is about and appreciating more the work and efforts put by the student.

The impact of a student staying regularly in contact with their supervisor and getting approval at key points in the project should not be underestimated. So students should plan for these meetings and here are some important guidelines:

Ideally student should come to the meeting with evidence of progress from the previous meeting. This could be by showing what sections have been completed, the experiment so far, design of questionnaires, or anything that would help the supervisor appreciate the progress on the project so far.

Student should come with set of prepared questions and clarifications regarding the work. There are many instances in this book in which we recommend students to double check or confirm these with their supervisor.

Student should take notes in the meeting. We recommend student write minutes of the meeting that would outline the key points discussed in the including what 'tasks' or 'actions' you are required to complete.

The student to agree with the supervisor what the next set of tasks will be including when the next meeting will take place.

Where possible, we recommend the student to type the minutes of the meeting and email these to the supervisor with the request to 'confirm' them. Supervisors will usually welcome these as they tend to create their own records of meetings as well.

1.6: How to read this book:

There are three approaches to reading this book for the purpose of completing the project thesis.

1. Reading the whole book before starting: This is recommended as it gives students a full overview of everything and will significantly save them time in avoiding mistakes later. However, students may sometimes forget details related to specific sections of their project. Plus it is not always possible to have the time to do so.

2. Read the chapters based on the writing up phase: This helps students know what they need to do as they progress from one chapter to another, they read what is needed to do next. However, this may result in mistakes that are only spotted later and missing the 'big' picture behind the project.

3. Combination of the first two: Read the whole book first then students to go back to each phase and review what they are supposed to do. This represents the ideal plan and minimizes mistake and will very likely save student time in making sure they get their work done in time.

Should the student decide to write their project based on the 10 phases listed earlier, then we recommend they review these sections of the book at each phase:

Phase 1: Review sections 1 & 8

Phase 2: Review sections 9 & 15

Phase 3: Review section 10

Phase 4: Review section 11

Phase 5: Review section 12

Phase 6: Review sections 13 & 14

Phase 7: Review sections 1 & 8

Phase 8: Review sections 3 & 6

Phase 9: Review sections 4, 5, & 7

Phase 10: Review section 2

1.7: Introduction and conclusion for every chapter

The writing up of the project requires that each chapter has its own introduction and conclusion. Students sometimes puzzle at this wandering what to write in each of these sections. Introductions and conclusions for each chapter need not be difficult or complicated.

Induction: To tell the readers what they are going to expect to find in this chapter. Many clues are given for the students in this book. For example, writing an introduction for the chapter titled: Chapter 1 Introduction would be tell the readers that this chapter will introduce them to the project and present the project aim, objectives, relate to how these objectives will be achieved and how the document is going to be laid out.

Conclusion: To reaffirm what the readers have covered in this chapter and relate the content to this chapter to what the readers are going to read in the next chapter.

So a conclusion to chapter one: Introduction would be confirm that the project title, aims, objectives, and project layout have been presented in a way the sets the stage to starting the research aspects of the project (the next chapter).

Section 2. Project Front Page

Usually a front page of a project should contain: a project title, name of the student, the name of the university (sometimes a logo), and the term/year it is submitted. The institution may have its own style and this should be found in the handbook or syllabus provided to students when they start their project. Examples of front pages:

Figure 1: Example of Front Page

UNIVERSITY of EAST LONDON

School of Computing, Information Technology, and Engineering

CN3061: Final Year Project

Semester A, 2011

u0955826

Figure 2: Example of Front page 2

Final Year Project Thesis

If the institution does not have a standard front project page, then we recommend the student to develop one for their project following these guidelines:

Project Title:
Sub title

Author's name

University
Logo

Name of the University
Name of School

Date and year

Figure 3: Front Page Template

Section 3. Abstract & Keywords

3.1. Abstract:

The abstract is a summary of the whole project. Abstract is sometimes called synopsis. In around 500 words or less, a student needs to tell the readers briefly about their project. A person who reads the abstract should be able to find the answers for three key questions:

- What is the project about?

- How did the student conduct the project?

- What is/are the outcome(s) of the project?

Of course 500 words means a student needs to summarize a lot. It is one of the reasons why abstract is only added after all the other parts of the project are completed. This is one of the reasons we recommended it near the end of the project.

An abstract should NOT:

- Exceed one page.

- Talk about problems students faced.

- Talk about personal issues.

\-   Include images or graphs.

Read the following abstracts and try to identify if anything is missing?

Abstract

With the development of information society in the form of social media, blogs, forum and social networks as a communication means, this is increasingly playing indispensable roles in people's daily life and it has been developing at a great speed which leads the influence on the whole academic life. Social media becomes the useful tool of teaching, studying and learning and it makes information transformation more frequently than before.

In this project, we will analyze the positive and negative affection of social media as a learning tool. Our project includes the overview of social media and the overview of academic life. This is followed by research background, research data, and the feedback of the research that provides new insights into use and possible future development in social media.

Figure 4: Abstract Example 1

1. Abstract

This report investigates the type of Internet capabilities, bandwidth and the trend in Internet usage in Nigeria. The report goes on to study the IT market to create a portal for online advertising. The analysis and design of a system focuses on web and data integrity including how it is implemented. The design recommends a server side technology that meets the requirements of the web standards. A suitable database system that captures data in real-time is implemented.

In addition, the research looks at the ethical and social issues relating to the project. The project concludes with a usability and accessibility evaluation of the website.

Figure 5: Abstract Example 2

Abstract

The concept of paperless classroom and utilizing e-learning technology to complement traditional learning is not a new idea. While some papers carried out an investigation to consider the use and the implication of such a switch on the student achievements, no papers could be found that attempts quantitative cost benefit analysis of such a switch. This paper presents an investigation carried out on four courses at a London university over a period of six years between 2006 and 2012 as they made the switch from paper-based, to paperless delivery, and then to complete Green Courses. A Green Course is a term used to describe a course that goes beyond paperless delivery to include processing of assessments, marking, and feedback in a completely paperless mood (Safieddine, & Wee Lee, 2013). This paper considers what formula educational institutes can use to calculate the cost benefit of implementing a Green Course. The proposed formula used considers the cost benefit for staff, students, and the university. The application of the formula identifies varying levels of costs and benefits for each category. The study showed that the overall savings collectively accumulated by the institution, staff and students can be considerably high, as much as £3million (or $4.5million) a year for an institution like University of East London (United Kingdom). However, our research identified some health and well-being costs that could not be quantified and should be subject of further research in this area.

Figure 6: Abstract Example 3

Some universities do not allow students to include citations in the abstract while other universities allow students to do so. Students should check with their supervisor what the university protocol on this is.

One approach to writing the abstract is to write one sentence from each chapter/section in the report. This way the student builds a full picture of the paper.

3.2. Executive Summary:

Some courses will require students to write 'Executive Summary'. Executive summary of a project has some similarities with abstract but also difference. Executive summary comes from the business practice of giving executives a brief outline of the main points in a report. This includes showing where in the report to find more detailed information.

Executive summary can extend to several pages for long reports and include headings and bullet points.

Despite the ability to extend the report to few pages, the report has to remain short and without too much detail. It should provide a commentary on the main points only and follow the layout of the report itself.

Similar the abstract, the executive summary is usually located at the start of the project should be written after the report is completed.

3.3. Keywords:

Finally, note that some courses may require students to include keywords in this section. Keywords are as the name indicates, the words that are key at defining what the main theme of this project is. The purpose of keywords is help readers get a quick ideas as to what the project domain. There is also a suggestion that with many project filed as 'electronic' copies, keywords can help in searching and finding the project by prospective researchers and students. Below are two examples of abstract followed by keywords to help students appreciate their use.

Abstract

The concept of paperless classroom and utilizing e-learning technology to complement or support traditional learning are not a new idea. However, very few papers, if any, carried out a longitude investigation to consider the implication of such a switch towards the students' achievement and experience of such a switch. This paper present an investigation carried out on four modules at School of Architecture, Computing and Engineering (ACE) of University of East London over a period of six years as they made the switch from paper-based, to paperless delivery, and then to complete green module. A green module is a term the authors define a module that goes beyond paperless delivery to include collection of assessments, marking, and feedback in a completely paperless mood. This paper conducts an in depth reviews of four green modules with review of the implication of such a switch. This paper also considers what method educational institutes can use to implement a Green Module. In the long term, the results show statistically significant improvement in students' performance, statistically significant progression and improved students' satisfaction. However, the study also shows that some modules that made a sudden switch rather than having an intermediate stage experienced short term drop in students' performance. Finally the paper examines limitations of the research and further research into this area.

Keywords: *Green Module, Paperless, Education, Student Experience, Virtual Learning Environment (VLE).*

Figure 7: Abstract & Keywords Example 1

Abstract

Many students struggle with mathematics as a subject and some become dissatisfied as they continually confront obstacles in subject engagement. The authors propose the introduction of Cooperative Active Learning methodology for Mathematics classes. The method would get students engage in groups of three or more when learning. Cooperative-learning techniques suggested here would employ formally structured groups of students assigned to complex tasks, such as multiple-step exercises, research projects, or presentations part of the mathematics lesson plans. The proposed method is based on cooperation between students with different levels with the main objective of this method is to increase the students' engagement, provide peer support, and improve passing rates.

Keywords: *cooperative learning, mathematics pedagogy, active learning, Dale cone, Bloom's taxonomy.*

Figure 8: Abstract & Keywords Example 2

Section 4. List of Contents

This is a table that lists the sections and chapters of the project with page numbers. Students are recommended to use the MS Word automatic-"table of contents" generator as it is easier to maintain and much more accurate. To be able to use MS Word auto-generated tables, students have to use Titles and Sub-Titles formats.

Chapters, sections and sub sections should be clearly numbered according to chapter number.

Example:

Chapter 2:...
    2.1...
    2.2....
        2.2.1...
        2.2.2.....
            2.2.2.1......
        2.2.3....
    2.3....
    2.4...

Chapter 3:....

Table of Content:

Chapter One: Introduction

1.1.Introduction and research rationale: 2
1.2.Outline of the research methodology: 5
1.3.Research Title: 8
  1.3.1. Research Aim: 8
  1.3.2. Research Objectives: 8
1.4.The organization of this thesis: 9

Chapter Two: Methodology

2.1. Introduction: 12
2.2. Research hypotheses and hypothesis-test: 12
2.3. Justification of the methodology: 14
2.4. Overview of research timeline: 14
2.5. Evaluation of the methodology: 17
2.6. Summary and Conclusion 18

Chapter Three: Literature Review

3.1. Introduction: 23
3.2. Electronic Commerce Web applications: 23
  3.2.1. Definitions of Electronic commerce: 23
  3.2.2. Characteristics of E-commerce Web applications: 26
3.3. Fourth generation Web programming languages: 28
  3.3.1. Categories of 4GL Web application packages: 30
3.4. Current literature on Web Modelling Languages: 32
  3.4.1. Structured Web modelling languages: 32
    3.4.1.1. Relationship Management Methodology (RMM): 32
    3.4.1.2. Araneus Project: 34
    3.4.1.3. Entity Relationship Models for Information Artefacts (ERMIA): 35
    3.4.1.4. Summary of structured Web modelling languages: 36
  3.4.2. Object-Oriented based Web modelling languages: 36
    3.4.2.1. The Object-Oriented Hypermedia Design Method (OOHDM): 37
    3.4.2.2. HyDev Approach: 38
    3.4.2.3. The Extended Unified Modelling Language: 39
    3.4.2.4. Summary of Object Oriented Modelling tools: 40
  3.4.3. Hypermedia and other Web modelling languages: 41
    3.4.3.1. Lite-Hypermedia Design Modelling (HDM-lite): 41
    3.4.3.2. Web Modelling Language (WebML): 42
    3.4.3.3. Dexter Modelling and Z notations: 43
    3.4.3.4. The Web Site Development Method (WSDM): 44

Figure 9: Example of Table of Content

It is recommended students learn how to set up their paper style before they write the project to save time formatting and editing nearer to the deadline.

Here is how to set the text styles of the project using MS Word.

Locate the 'styles' option from the 'Home' tab. From that option, the student can have full view of all the style clicking on the corner of the scroll bar of the 'styles' section.

Figure 10: Finding the 'Styles' of the document

Few key terms to make note of: 'Normal' is for the text across the document. 'Title' is usually used for project title. 'Heading 1' is usually used for chapter titles, and 'Heading 2, 3, 4…' for the sub titles. If we apply these styles to the sections we showed earlier, they may change to look something like this:

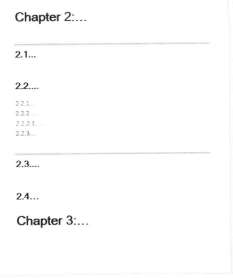

Figure 11: Example of heading styles

It is once all the titles, heading, and sub heading, MS Word are set that the student can generate the table of content for their project faster and easier. To generate it, click on 'References' tab and select the 'Table of Contents' section. MS word will give students options on what the table of content should looks like and they can choose the one that suits them.

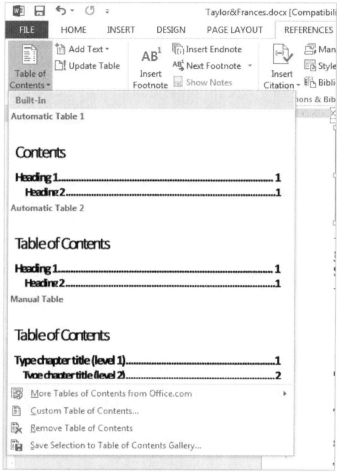

Figure 12: Selecting table of content style

On selecting the style needed, MS Word will generate the table of content automatically for the students.

Students are recommended to ask their supervisor if there is a standard text style the university. Some universities provide a MS Word document with the style pre-set for consistency.

Section 5. List of Figures and Tables

The following lists tend to be optional. If the student is going to have Figures, Diagrams, Tables, Formulas, or anything that needs to have caption, then these need to be numbered independently from reach other. Students should create a list of them at the front of the thesis after the Table of Contents.

List of Figures:

If there are going to be figures or diagrams in the project, then the student needs to have a table that lists them.

List of Tables:

If there is going to be tables in the project thesis, the student needs to be number them also.

Look closely at the example in figure 3, and notice the naming and numbering helps readers to quickly locate what they are looking for. The first number indicates the chapter number then item number. Example: Table 5.2 is the second table in chapter 5.

List of Tables:

List of Equations:

Figure 13: Other types of lists

Notice in figure 3 there is a list of equations. Again depending on the project or student's need, these could be included to.

MS Word allows users to create these lists from the 'Reference' Tab. Students can make use of this early on in the writing of their project to speed up the generation of their list of figures, equations, and tables. For each time student adds a table, equation, or figure, they should select 'Insert Caption' from the 'References' tab. A pop up menu called 'Caption' will appear allowing students to select what type of caption they are adding: figure, table and equation.

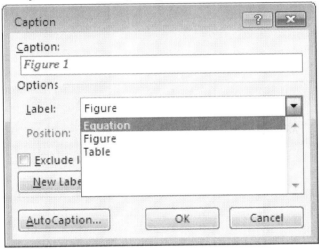

Figure 14: Inserting Captions

By selecting all the correction captions for the document, MS word will generate these lists by selecting 'Insert Table of Figures'

Section 6. Acknowledgement

It is the student's chance to thank people who have supported them in doing the project. This may include companies and individuals who participated in the project, people who guided them and encouraged them during the studies and completing their final year project. Mentioning supervisor(s), friends, and family is very common.

This acknowledgement has to be short, no more than 300 words. Refrain from writing long lists of people. Do not make a mistake few students have done in the past by mentioning fellow students who 'helped' them write the project. This is cheating as the project is supposed to be the sole work of the student.

Many assessors will read this section to get a better idea as to who are the contributors in this project.

Getting support and encouragement is different than getting help. Here are examples:

Acknowledgements

This work is dedicated to my father, XXXX XXXX XXXX (RIP) for his love forgiving nature.

I will like to thank Mike Kretsis for his patience and good tutorship and Dr. F. Safieddine for his immense knowledge and contribution and especially his guidance.

Figure 15: Example of Acknowledgement 1

Acknowledgement

I would like to express my deep gratitude to friends and family who supported me when I started this project. In addition, I also would like to thank my project supervisor for the support and advice giving to me during the execution of this project.

Figure 16: Example of Acknowledgement 2

Acknowledgement

I would like to take this opportunity to acknowledge all the people who have guided and supported me in completing this project; I will start by thanking my supervisor Dr. Fadi Safieddine who remained patient with me during the course of the research phase of this project. His guidance has helped put my mind back to focus on the actual procedures, your strength and guidance has given me confidence to have belief in myself.

I would like to say a big thanks to my Course Leader Mr. Mike Kretsis and my tutorial tutor for their diligence and hard work in making sure that the content and core issues of this module are understood. I will also like to thank my friends for the sleepless nights at the flat. Finally, I would like to thank Royal Docks Company for allowing me to conduct my research at their premises and for giving me access to the data required for my research.

Figure 17: Example of Acknowledgement 3

Students will notice from these three examples that the text has to be short and clear.

Section 7. Definition of Terms

This section is only applicable if the student believes that there are several terms or abbreviations used in the content of the project thesis that may be confusing and will require readers at times to revisit their definitions. Do not assume the supervisor knows everything about the topic or that he/she will be the only person who will read the work. It is standard academic practice for final year projects on all levels to be checked and graded by two academics. One of the people who will grade the project is the supervisor but the other one will not necessarily be someone who is a specialist in the subject of the project.

Students should sort the terms in alphabetic order. Emphasize the word or abbreviation and include after each term a very short definition.

Glossary:

Applet: is a small application that can be attached to a Web site and can be reused. Examples of Applets are: Chat rooms, forums, search engines, and online games.

CASE tool: stands for Computer Assisted Software Engineering. CASE tool is a program that assists users in creating the code from the design models. In Web context, CASE tools are used to create prototypes of the Web application.

Cookie: is a small text file that is stored on the user's computer by the Web site with information regarding user's visit. This allows the Web site to identify the user and customize both presentation and/or functionalities.

Forms: are also called HTML Forms. These forms allow Web pages to take input from users. Examples of forms: Email forms, feedback forms, and order forms.

Frame: is the condition where a Web page is divided into at least two sections: index and target. Allows a Web page to be built from several Web pages.

Hyperlinks: are small instructions that create a link between two pages or an anchor link within the Web page.

Hypermedia: is an application based on pages with hyperlinks that allow linking from one page to the other. Examples of hypermedia are: Web sites, multimedia CD-ROMs, and hypertext application screens.

Figure 18: Example of definition of terms

Standard academic practices still apply here, which means students should not copy definitions from other sources without referencing. They should express these definitions in their own words.

Section 8. Chapter One :Introduction

This chapter would represent an elaborated version of the project abstract. It would contain explanation of the nature of the project, scope of the project, and structure of the project. However, students should not include any mentioning of results. This chapter should contain the following sections: Introduction, Project Title, Project Aim and Objectives, Project Tasks, and explanation of project documentation structure.

Student would be forgiven for thinking this is the first chapter they write. While students may create a skeleton version of it at the start, they will not finish this chapter until the very end. Some students will write an outline focusing on the "aims and objectives" and leave everything else till after they finish the project. Students cannot be sure what all the project tasks or final document structure is going to be until they finish it.

It is important here to emphasize the difference between "Aim" and "Objectives", as they are not the same. Aim tends to be one statement stating exactly what student wants to achieve: "Design a car that is more eco-friendly." Objectives tend to be several statements that show all essential steps needed to achieve the aim where if one of these objectives are missed, the student would fail to achieve the whole project "Aim". So for the aim listed above, these could be the "Objectives":

1. *To research current engine models.*

2. *To set criteria for petrol consumption.*

3. *To design car outlining petrol consumption reductions.*

4. *To conduct experiments on a given model.*

5. *To evaluate outcome of the experiment against existing models.*

With project thesis objective, we recommend students to consider some of the key terms that most project thesis should have:

- "Research": this could refer to the review of the literature, researching latest methods, and/or reading what other people have done.
- "Design": this could refer to planning or outlining a way to do the project.
- "Conduct" or "implement": this could refer to how the project is applied in a way the produced an outcome.

- "Evaluate": this would refer to reflection on the success of the work and what has been learned from this project.

Some supervisors may require students to explain how they intend to achieve these objectives. This is merely to ensure that these objectives are achievable.

It is good practice to have a 'chapter front page' with each chapter. It welcomes readers. Also students should have an introduction and conclusion for each chapter. This might sound odd but even for chapter one students should have an introduction to their introduction. Introductions do not need to be too complicated, as they just need to tell the reader what they are about to read in this chapter. Conclusions could simply summarize what they reviewed in that chapter.

Chapter One: Introduction

Figure 19: Example of a Front Cover of a chapter

Section 9. Chapter Two: Literature Review

This chapter represents a review of everything the student read and is directly related to the project. This would come from books, journals, conference papers, research papers, newspapers, handbooks, or course work reviewed as part of the project. In short, this chapter should present everything the student is using as bases for their project. This includes issues like: current publications/views related to the projects, current technology the student is using to do their project, modeling tools/programming languages they investigated in the process of choosing their project, research techniques, and/or issues directly on indirectly related to the successful operation of the product produced as part of the project. Two things students should remember carefully about this chapter: Everything they present should be backed with an in-text reference. Other than the introduction and conclusion for this chapter, every paragraph has to have at least one reference. There are two common ways for in-text citations: Author/Date in-text citations and Numeric citations. The most common in project thesis publications is the Author/Date in-text citations.

teachers showed that participants had positive attitudes towards learner-centered instruction and its potential to make education engaging, enjoyable, involving, challenging, and relevant to students' learning (Yilmaz, 2008).

Based on the work of Weimer (2002), this conceptual work suggests a practical model for the implementation of the learner centered approach in the Arabian Gulf region. As a matter of fact, despite the existence of extensive research on the usefulness and practicability of learner centered approach, few studies have offered a comprehensive model with clear guidance and examples on how such an approach could be implemented, particularly in Middle Eastern context. The observations and experiments of two business professors with collective experience of 25 years in higher education has helped generate various propositions that will be presented throughout this manuscript. Those practical propositions revolves around the five pillars of Weimer (2002)'s framework.

In defining the topic, Weimer (2002) suggests that Learner Centered teaching"... involves a reallocation of power in the classroom. It requires that faculty share with students some control over those learning processes that directly affect them" (Weimer, 2002, p.45). Furthermore, Stage (1998) summarizes the Learner Centered approach as "Constructivist approaches emphasize learners' actively constructing their own knowledge rather than passively receiving information transmitted to them from teachers and textbook" (Stage et al., 1998, p.35).

Blumberg and Pontiggia (2011) proposed a four-staged model to represent the transition from instructor-centered teaching to learner-centered approach. Two intermediate levels are in the middle: lower-level of transition and higher-level of transition. Warring (2010) applied Hersey & Blanchard situational leadership model to develop a four-staged model of independence:

Figure 20: In-text Referencing (Author/Date)

The Author/Date in-text citation is usually requested for institutions that require students to follow the APA, Harvard, Chicago, and Turabian referencing style. The Numeric in-text citation is requested for institutions that require students to follow MLA or Oxford referencing style.

2 Literature Review

Oxford Internet Survey of 2013 results show online social networks as becoming one of the key sources of information and news especially among younger generations [6]. Thus, the spread of misinformation has increased as a result of the increase in the number of people using social networks [7]. Due to the lack of accountability of social media users spreading information and not having appropriate filtering techniques similar to reviewing and editing information in traditional publishing, social media have become a significant media for the spread of misinformation [4]. Thus, the spread of diverse forms of information, misinformation, and propaganda involves the distribution of false information through an information diffusion process involving users of social networks where the majority of users may not be attentive to the untruth story. In one study, researchers state that the acceptance of misleading information by the people greatly depends on their prior beliefs and opinions [8]. In another study [9], researchers state that the spread of misinformation in online social networks is context specific with topics such as health, politics, finances, theology, and technology trends are key sources of misinformation. People believe things which support their past thoughts without questioning them [10]. We have used the term misinformation to denote any type of false information spreading in social networks.

Figure 21: In-text Referencing (Numeric)

Notice how each paragraph, for each topic, there is a reference. MS Word has a feature that allows student to create in-text citation that would later generate the 'end of project' reference list. From the 'Reference' tab, students could use the 'Insert Citation' based on the reference style recommended by their institution.

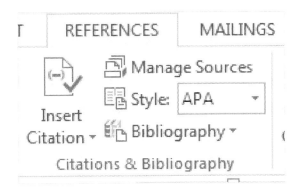

Figure 22: MS Word to insert citation

Also notice that the student's opinion as the author are not presented. The student is allowed to explain issues such as differences, similarities, or opposing views but they should try to find references for these as well.

This chapter represents "other people's" research, publications, and work that are related to the project. This will likely be the biggest chapter in the project. Depending on the subject, literature reviews can be as much as 60% of the whole document. Also it is the first chapter to start working on. As soon as the topic is agreed with the supervisor, the work starts at researching the subject even if the student has believe they 'know everything they need to know' about the project, the readers of their project need to see this in the literature review. Students should do all their review of the literature before they proceed to the following stages.

When sourcing information, students are required to paraphrase that information into their literature review. Students should refrain from copying text and using 'quotes' unless the content of the quote is significant in it attribute to the subject and the author. Bad practices here are when students do not reference their literature review or simply copy/paste text as 'quotes' across the document.

The last issue remaining is getting the right sources. The literature review should present variety of sources and variety of opinions and views. But how to judge reliable sources? There is generally a view that not all sources of information are equal. Here is a list, based purely on the opinion of the author of this book, which goes from highly reliable to least reliable. Students should check with their supervisor for their view on what they consider reliable and less reliable.

- Academic Journals (Highly Reliable): if student is going to base a key part of their argument on a source, then they need to also consider the type and credentials of that journal.
- Academic Text books (Highly Reliable): if this text book is defined for a course and is published by a reputable publishing house then this can be highly reliable source.
- Refereed Conference Publications (Reliable): Where is a well-known conference and where the proceedings have impact factor, then students could use these are reliable sources.
- Company reports, Government report, and not published reports (less reliable): the problem with these reports is that they may have not been vetted and checked. Students are allowed to use these but with caution.
- Wikipedia (less reliable): while some research suggest the new and very strict vetting of

Wikipedia of its content makes it as reliable as many academic publications, the consensus is that it is not very reliable. However, where a student finds a key information or facts they wish to use, Wikipedia provides sources of their information which presents and excellent way to verify this information further.
- Other sources (not reliable): Websites, magazines, newspapers, and other sources of information are generally considered not reliable. However, for 'events' and where the information has been reported in more than one major news agency and verified, then this could be taken as reliable. Reasoning and authentication plays an important role here in order to include some of these sources in the project.

These may seem like a tough criteria to follow but generally academics do not like to see many websites as references and students should be treating these sources as unquestionably facts.

Section 10. Chapter Three: Case Study

This chapter represents the student's opportunity to elaborate on the case study he/she is using as part of the project. It is optional as not all project thesis have a case study. Some may have multiple case studies, in which case they all have to be included in this chapter and the title of this chapter changed to 'Case Studies". Students should ask permission using a company as a case study. Some universities will require students to complete permission to visit or conduct research outside the university in order to comply with health and safety regulations. Students should refrain from putting individual names unless explicit permission is obtained. In many instances, the name of the company could be used and roles of individuals explained without mentioning names.

Different courses will have specific expectations from this section. Business courses will require students to create 'Organizational Chart' of the management hierarchy, system/process structure, or any diagrams that would facilitate the understanding of the case. While research projects in science will require students to discuss the demographics and sampling characteristics of their case study.

Case studies do not have to be companies or organizations. They could be medical or experimental case studies. In whatever discipline the students are studying, they should make sure the supervisor approves their case study as there maybe ethical and legal considerations that need to be addressed before they start.

Students should keep this chapter as short as possible. Students should not overload this chapter with too much detail. Specimens of documentations, log meetings, interviews, or other paperwork need not be placed in this chapter but left for the appendix.

Students discussing or using documents from an experiment or company should make sure they have permissions and rights to report these in their project. Getting the line manager to sign under the document indicating 'permission to use in research thesis' with date maybe sufficient. Students should be aware that names and details of customers, employees, and individuals are subject to 'data protection act' and should not be used in research without permission of these individuals.

Section 11. Chapter Four: Methodology

This is an essential chapter which students need to have in one form or another. Some other names this chapter could go by are: method, approach, or process. The methodology chapter in principle should explain how the student is about to conduct their research, experiment, and/or project. Of course there are more than one way to do a project. A practical computing IT project methodology, for instance, would require students to consider project methods such as Waterfall, RAD, XP, Agile, or Prince 2 as a project methodology. Research projects will require students to consider methods such as: Quantitative, Qualitative, Correlation / Regression analysis, or Meta-Analysis. Students should be familiar with the meaning of these terms as they are generic and apply to a wide variety of programmes:

- **Qualitative Research:** A research-based project that use interview techniques, surveys, focus groups, and observations for a small sample of individuals. Qualitative Research is mainly investigative research. It is used to understand reasons, opinions, and motivations behind facts or events and starts with a 'research question' or a 'hypothesis'.

- **Quantitative Research:** A type of research based on analysis of data involving numerical and statistical explanations. Quantitative research aims at quantifying attitudes, opinions, behaviours, and other defined variables to generalize results from a larger sample population. Some of the techniques used in quantitative research include face-to-face interviews, telephone interviews, longitudinal studies, website interceptors, online polls, and systematic observations.
- **Regression or Correlation Analysis:** A research method that attempts to identify relationships between two different variables. This would help understand the underlying relations between these. Example increase sale of ice cream with increase in temperature.
- **Meta-Analysis:** probably the most difficult of research methods. It requires studying other research papers and projects with the aim to cover every publication possible in order to get an average impact of several of these papers.

Of course there are many other disciplines and many other methods. In this chapter, the student should aim to clarify what research or implementation methods are available and which one of these did the student choose for their project.

Students should remember to keep this chapter short and 'lecture' free. Explaining the different techniques in conducting the project should be done in chapter two: 'Literature review'. In this chapter, students need to just show the steps they have taken to do the project.

There are instances where students maybe required to explain why they selected one technique as opposed to another technique. When comparing different ways of doing the project, students need to list the advantages and disadvantages of each method.

Getting the methodology correct is not always easy. We recommend students to review what previous students have done and always make sure their supervisor approves the methodology before implementing it.

Section 12. Chapter Five: Implementation

In this chapter students are required to explain the outcomes of their project thesis as <u>objectively</u> as possible. In other terms, students should present their project findings as facts, screen shots of their work, summary of questionnaire results, summary of interview answers, experiment outcome, or anything that resulted from their project that does not involve <u>analysis </u>of the outcomes. Students should not state their opinion, nor should they include details from their literature review. Implementation chapter should be in a summarized form. Highlighting the successful and unsuccessful aspects of the project would come in the next chapter. Students are encouraged to use screen shots and result tables.

Where a project did not meet all its objectives or did not get completed successfully, students should make sure these are shown.

Students should not try to cover up mistakes. In academic context, learning from a failed project is sometimes as valuable as learning from a successful experiment.

Other than 'implementation' this chapter maybe also

called: Results or outcomes. Depending on the size of the project and the amount of results, some students may combine this chapter with the next chapter resulting in one chapter called "Implementation and Evaluation" or "Results and Analysis". We do not encourage this as it may distort what is the outcome with what is the students' evaluation of that outcome.

Section 13. Chapter Six: Evaluation

It is in this section that a student would state their evaluation of their project. Evaluations are supposed to be unbiased and honest. Students are recommended to start by stating important outcomes of their project. What interesting stuff did the student discover from the experiment? What new facts did the survey show? What important features did the program they created do? Other names given sometimes to this chapter are: Analysis, Findings, Reflection, Assessment, or Outcomes. Ultimately, the aim is for the student to analyze the outcome of their work in an unbiased way.

Then students need to consider what aspects of their project turned out to be less interesting or unsuccessful. Students should never try to cover up mistakes, problems, or incomplete work. Supervisors and examiners tend to be aware that projects do not always run smoothly and, of course, there will be glitches. Students should not start complaining and blaming everyone and everything. This is not the chapter for it. How bad these glitches are and how much of it is the student's responsibility is something that is hard to judge.

Supervisors tend to focus on the students' aim and objectives agreed at the start of the semester and found in chapter one. The aim and objectives are set out to be achievable and therefore supervisors expect the student to be able to achieve them, even if not perfectly. Therefore, it is advisable that the aim and objectives make out a specific section in this chapter where students present facts that would back the view that they have met these. This will help readers appreciate if the student is justified in their claim that they have been successful or otherwise.

Section 14. Chapter Seven: Conclusion

This is one of those chapters that regularly get overlooked by students or rushed with failure to appreciate its' importance. Not only do supervisors read it with interest, it usually has significant grade associated with it. Here students have a chance to put some personal prospective on how the project ran. They could reflect on their personal experience in developing and writing their project. Any bad luck, mistakes, problems, or difficulties could be listed but in the context of "Learn from my experience" or "Do not do the mistakes I did!" This chapter should not turn out to be a blaming failures on everyone or a long list of bad lucks. Supervisors, who have far more experience than the student, having done many projects before they became lecturers understand that projects do not always go smoothly. But they can also distinguish between those committed students who attended their meetings and worked hard but had a bit of bad luck from those students who hardly ever showed up, did not do any of the work during the term, and tried to do everything in the last two weeks yet now they want to blame everyone but themselves.

On the other hand, students should avoid turning

this section into a 'Self-congratulating' by trying to cover up mistakes by suggesting that the project is a 'huge' success, flawless, and no one in the world can do it better! Students need to be honest in their reflection as to how the has been conducted and what they have learned. There is always room for improvements, repeating the research in a better way, or following up the research with ideas for future research.

A very important section in the conclusion is "recommendation" which would reflect on what would anyone who decides to do the same or similar project should do. What have the student learned that would benefit other people?

Common sub-titles expected in this chapter are: reflection on aims and objects, learning experience from the project, problems encountered during developing the project, further research, and recommendations.

Section 15. Bibliography / References

This section should contain all sources of information that were used in the process of building the project and writing the research part. It is important that the student include all reference to quotes or information collected from external sources in their document. Please refer to the project handbook or syllabus for the method of recording bibliography. Universities differ as to what style of referencing they require, Harvard, APA, Chicago, and MLA being the four most popular ones. Refer to the end of this book for examples of how these different 'references' look like in the section "How to reference this book".

Citations in the project text and having end of project 'Bibliography' or 'References' is absolutely essential. Here the student need to check with the project supervisor what the university requires students to use as there is a small difference between 'Bibliography' and 'References'. With Bibliography, students will put the references to everything they cited in the document and they read part of writing the project. With 'References', the focus is only on sources that are cited in the document. For example, take the reading of this book part of the students' research into project thesis. This book should be included in a bibliography but not in the references unless the students has directly cited something from the book.

The process of writing the end of project references or bibliography starts from the moment the project topic, aims and objectives are approved. Failure to do so will result in significant delays near the end of the project.

Supervisors will check how the project presents citations and references carefully as it demonstrates an essential skill in academic writing. Where a supervisor finds far less number of references and citations, they immediately suspect plagiarism. As explain before, the literature review chapter, which is the biggest chapter, has to be cited at every stage.

There are many websites that can help students generate references provided they record all the information needed. These websites tend to generate one reference at a time and are as good as the information provided.

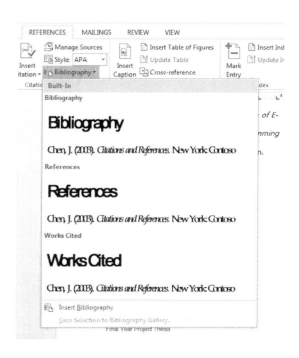

Figure 23: MS Word Auto generated references

However, if the student has followed our advice in section 9, then they would be able to generate their list of references quite easily using the auto-generate Bibliography / References in MS Word. This option is found in the 'References' tab.

Notice here there are several ways to writing the references/bibliography section which corresponds to the in-text referencing mentioned in section 9. Where the in-text referencing is Author/date, then the end of project document reference/bibliography is Author/Date in alphabetic order. If, however, the in-text referencing is a number, then naturally the end of project document reference/bibliography is

listed by their reference number in numeric order.

Adams, W. J., and Jansen, J. (1998). Information technology and the classroom of the future. In *Society for Information Technology & Teacher Education International Conference* (Vol. 1998, No. 1, pp. 484-488).

Awedh, M., Mueen,. A, Zafar, B. and Manzoor, U (2014) Using Socrative and Smartphones for the support of collaborative learning. *International Journal on Integrating Technology in Education*. Vol3. Number 4. pp. 18-24.

Bayliss, L., Connel, C., Farmer, W. (2012) Effects of ebook readers and tablet computers on reading comprehension. *Journal of Instructional Media*, 39(2), pp. 131-140

Bonastre, O.M., Benavent, A.P., and Belmonte, F.N., (2006) Pedagogical Use of Tablet PC for Active and Collaborative Learning. *IEEE Professional Communication Society 2006 proceedings*, pp. 214-218.

Cassidy, E. D., Colmenares, A., Jones, G., Manolovitz, T., Shen, L., & Vieira, S., (2014) Higher Education and Emerging Technologies: Shifting Trends in Student Usage. *Journal of Academic Librarianship*. Mar2014, Vol. 40 Issue 2, p124-133.

Corbeil, J.R. and Valdes-Corbeil, M.E. (2007) Are You Ready for Mobile Learning? Educause Review. Printed 1ˢᵗ of January 2007. Retrieved from: https://net.educause.edu/ir/library/pdf/EQM0726.pdf

Daccord, T., and Reich, J., (2015) *How to Transform Teaching with Tablets*. Educational Leadership. May2015, Vol. 72 Issue 8, p18-23. 6p.

Figure 24: References (Author/Date)

1. Lee, K., Mahmud, J., Chen, J., Zhou, M., Nichols, J.: Who will retweet this?: Automatically identifying and engaging strangers on twitter to spread information. In: The 19th international conference on Intelligent User Interfaces, ACM, pp. 247-256 (2014)
2. Hoang, T. A., Lim, E. P.:Virality and Susceptibility in Information Diffusions. In: ICWSM (2012)
3. Jin, F., Dougherty, E., Saraf, P., Cao, Y., Ramakrishnan, N.: Epidemiological modeling of news and rumors on twitter. In: Proceedings of the 7th Workshop on Social Network Mining and Analysis, ACM. p.8 (2013)
4. Budak, C., Agrawal, D., El Abbadi, A.: Limiting the spread of misinformation in social networks. In: Proceedings of the 20th international conference on World Wide Web, ACM, pp. 665-674 (2011)
5. Safieddine, F., Masri, W., Pourghomi, P.: Corporate Responsibility in Combating Online Misinformation. International Journal of Advanced Computer Science and Applications(IJACSA), 7(2),pp. 126-132 (2016)
6. Dutton, W.H., Blank, G., Gorseli, D.: Cultures of the Internet: The Internet in Britain. Oxford Internet Survey 2013 Report: University of Oxford (2013)
7. World Economic Forum Report.: Top 10 trends of 2014: The rapid spread of misinformation online (2014)

Figure 25: Reference (Numeric)

Section 16. Appendix

Students can have several appendices depending on their project. Appendices would include bulk and large amount of material that examiners might be interested to view in the process of reading the project. Students should ask their supervisor what essential parts are required in the appendix. For example, one important appendix required by business and computing students is the 'Project Management'. Supervisors want to see the student demonstrating time and project management skills which may include Gantt chart, meeting logs, task management, and evidence of how the student managed his/her time while working on the project.

Section 17. Time Management

Time management maybe the one single most common reason why students fail their final year project on any level and in most courses. Students completing their final year project tend to still have final year courses, may have a lot on their mind regarding the three or four years they have invested in studying and may even be starting to look for job or next stage in their education. All these prove to be distractions that means students would not dedicate enough time to plan and manage their project successfully or get the grade they need. Having over 16 years in higher education, I have few important tips for prospective students. Break the project into phases and then into tasks. Students should keep track of the phase and what tasks they can do. The tasks can be done in any order they want but they should progress one task at a time. Every morning, students should pick a task. Break this task into sub tasks that could be done in one single day.

If a task proves to be too difficult or too long, then the task needs to be broken further. Take example the literature review chapter. This is a phase. Break this into tasks: Introduction, methods in designing cars, latest research into 'eco-friendly' cars, criteria to judge 'eco-friendly' cars, health and safety regulations, testing methods...etc. If student picks task 'Methods in designing cars' and they find this will require several days, they could break it into 'Reading about three methods of car designing' as one day task.

Students should regularly, say once a week, review the overall picture of the project and how it is progressing. Students should never shy from contacting their supervisors for clarifications and make sure of those regularly scheduled meeting with their supervisors.

Section 18. Presentation of Project

Not all final year projects require students to present their work but the majority do. There tends to be three very similar forms in which student present their final year project: the presentation format, the viva format, and combination of both.

The presentation format tends to be done in a form of a lecture or PowerPoint slides presentation. The student has to present a summary of their work, explaining the research, methodology, outcome and analysis in a limited time. Other forms of presentation include the outcome of the work such that done by architecture, computer programming, and engineering students.

The viva format tends to be done in a form of a panel meeting where the supervisor along with an examiner will want the student to summarize the work briefly and then answer series of questions about the project. Viva format could be tough and require students to be prepared having reviewed every part of the project. The term 'defend' the thesis is sometimes associated with final year viva in method where the examiner will question many aspects of the project and the student needs to be able to explain and justify aspects of their project.

The third format is probably the most popular in academia and it involves combination of a presentation and a viva. Students have to prepare a well-rehearsed presentation, demonstrate excellent understanding of the project and be prepared to defend their project.

Few tips a student needs to remember when preparing for their final year presentation. A student should demonstrate confidence in their subject and rehearse their presentation very well so their attention could be turned to the discussion part. If the student expects some questions to focus on a specific parts of their project such as limited or weak parts, then they need to come prepared beforehand with how they would defend these. If the student is unable to defend a part or feels the examiner has spotted a problem in their project, students need to stay calm and where possible acknowledge that this part needs improving. It is not unusual that students pass their final year project with requirements to make corrections or improvements.

Bibliography:

1. Citation Machine. (n.d.) Retrieved January 21, 2015, from www.citationmachine.net
2. Philips, E. (2000) How to get a PhD: a handbook for students and their supervisors. Open University Press. 3rd Edition.
3. Safieddine, F. (2004) Empirical Evaluation of E-commerce for fourth generation programming languages. PhD University of East London.

How to reference this book?

APA: - Safieddine, F. (2016) Student's guide for final year project thesis. (K.Lomidze, Ed) New York: CreativeSpace Publishing.

Harvard: - Safieddine, F, (2016) Student's guide for final year project thesis, ed. K Lomidze, New York: CreativeSpace Publishing.

MLA: - Safieddine, Fadi. Student's guide for final year project. Ed. Koba Lomidze. New York: CreativeSpace Publishing, 2016.

Chicago: - Safieddine, Fadi. Student's guide for final year project. Edited by Koba Lomidze. New York: CreativeSpace, 2016.

About the Author

Author: Dr. Fadi Safieddine (BSc, MSc, P.G.Cert, MBCS, PhD)

Associate Professor in MIS at the American University of the Middle East (AUM). Has strong background in statistics and management information systems. Completed his PhD from University of East London, and professional member of the British Computer Society (MBCS). Dr. Safieddine has over 16 years experience in higher education and has been involved in degree, masters, and PhD supervision. This book was developed initially to help his degree students appreciate the steps involved in writing up a project. The popularity of it and the difference they made have convinced him to make the book available for all students.

Editor:

Dr. Koba Lomidze (BA, MSe, PhD)

Assistant Professor at the American University of the Middle East (AUM). Currently teaches English Composition at the undergraduate level as assistant professor.

Has a PhD in Linguistics from Georgian Technical University (Tbilisi, Georgia) and a Master of Science in Education, International Higher Education Leadership from Old Dominion University (Virginia, USA).

Dr. Lomidze is passionate about the studies in second language acquisition.

Feedback:

We always welcome feedback for improvements. Please do not hesitate to contact us below:

Contact author: Dr Fadi Safieddine at www.fadi.me.uk or fadi@fadi.me.uk

Or contact editor at Lomidze@hotmail.com

27404285R00044

Printed in Great Britain
by Amazon